Beautiful Birds

COLORING BOOK

SIRIUS

SIRIUS

This edition published in 2021 by Sirius Publishing, a division of
Arcturus Publishing Limited,
26/27 Bickels Yard, 151–153 Bermondsey Street,
London SE1 3HA

ISBN: 978-1-83940-268-5
CH004982NT
Supplier 29, Date 0721, Print run 11676

Printed in China

Introduction

Birds have always been a source of fascination for many people—not only naturalists, but also those of us who just like to set up a bird table in the garden so we can watch their activities and admire their beauty. They are wonderful subjects to paint and draw, too, but difficult if you are not an experienced artist. You can photograph birds so you can study them at leisure, but finding out how to portray feathers and colors so that you can make them come alive on paper is another matter.

The answer is to learn from artists of the past, discovering how they captured the essence of the birds they painted. The plates in this book are taken from *A History of the Birds of Europe* (1871) by H E Dresser and *The Birds of America* (1840-44) by John T Bowen and John James Audubon. In the days before photography came of age, accurate, detailed paintings were the only way of providing a visual record of a species—but the artistry of Audubon's work rose far above a careful depiction of the subject for the benefit of scientists and appealed to the general public curious to know about the natural world.

Audubon often worked with watercolor, combining it with pastel to render the texture of feathers. You may find it easiest to start with colored pencils, though. By blending them you will be able to achieve the rich colors of the plates—but take care to follow the direction of the feathers as you work. For watercolor, you need only a small set of paints and a watercolor brush with a fine point—a No. 6 round brush is a good size to begin with. Thus equipped, you're ready to go. The delight of a coloring-in book is that you can get straight into applying colors without worrying about your drawing skills, safe in the knowledge that the outlines and features of your birds will look true to life.

Diana Vowles

Key: *List of plates*

1 Firecrest *(Regulus ignicapillus)* and goldcrest *(Regulus regulus)*

2 Waxwing *(Bombycilla garrulus)*

3 Western bluebird *(Sialia mexicana)*

4 Harris's buzzard, or Harris's hawk *(Parabuteo unicinctus)*

5 Common redstart *(Phoenicurus phoenicurus)*

6. Common kingfisher *(Alcedo atthis)*

7 Golden oriole *(Oriolus oriolus)*

8 Azure-winged magpie *(Cyanopica cyanus)*

9 Eagle owl *(Bubo bubo)*

10 Red-rumped swallow *(Cecropis daurica)*

11 Dalmatian pelican *(Pelicanus crispus)*

12 Black-headed bunting *(Emberiza melanocephala)*

13 Rose-coloured starling
(*Pastor roseus*)

14 Lazuli bunting
(*Passerina amoena*)

15 Common redpoll
(*Carduelis flammea*)

16 Pine grosbeak
(*Pinicola enucleator*)

17 Griffon vulture
(*Gyps fulvus*)

18 Northern cardinal
(*Cardinalis cardinalis*)

19 Greater flamingo
(*Phoenicopterus roseus*)

20 Common buttonquail
(*Turnix sylvaticus*)

21 Two-barred crossbill
(*Loxia leucoptera
bifasciata*) and white-
winged crossbill (*Loxia
leucoptera leucoptera*)

22 Swallow-tailed flycatcher
or scissor-tailed
flycatcher (*Tyrannus
forficatus*)

23 Common kestrel
(*Falco tinnunculus*)

24 Northern bullfinch
(*Pyrrhula pyrrhula
pyrrhula*)

25 American goldfinch
(Spinus tristis)

26 Brandt's jay
(Garrulus glandarius brandti)

27 Townsend's warbler
(Setophaga townsendi)

28 Common starling
(Sturnus vulgaris)

29 Long-eared owl
(Asio otus)

30 Steller's jay
(Cyanocitta stelleri)

31 Purple heron
(Ardea purpurea)

32 White-throated kingfisher
(Halcyon smyrnensis)

33 Hawfinch
(Coccothraustes coccothraustes)

34 Green woodpecker
(Picus viridis)

35 Golden-winged warbler
(Vermivora chrysoptera)

36 Red-backed shrike
(Lanius collurio)

37 Double-crested cormorant
(Phalacrocorax auritus)

38 Common wood pigeon
(Columba palumbus)

39 White-backed
woodpecker
(Dendrocopos leucotos)

40 Green-backed purple
gallinule *(Porphyrio
smaragdonotus)*

41 Scarlet tanager
(Piranga olivacea)

42 Caucasian great rosefinch
(Carpodacus rubicilla)

43 Savannah sparrow
*(Passerculus
sandwichensis)*

44 Greenfinch
(Carduelis chloris)

Regulus ignicapillus and *Regulus regulus*

Firecrest and goldcrest

Bombycilla garrulus

Waxwing

Sialia mexicana

Western bluebird

Parabuteo unicinctus

Harris's buzzard, or Harris's hawk

5

Phoenicurus phoenicurus

Common redstart

Alcedo atthis

Common kingfisher

Oriolus oriolus

Golden oriole

Cyanopica cyanus

Azure-winged magpie

Bubo bubo

Eagle owl

Cecropis daurica

Red-rumped swallow

Pelicanus crispus

Dalmatian pelican

Emberiza melanocephala

Black-headed bunting

Pastor roseus

Rose-coloured starling

Passerina amoena

Lazuli bunting

Carduelis flammea

Common redpoll

Pinicola enucleator

Pine grosbeak

Gyps fulvus

Griffon vulture

Cardinalis cardinalis

Northern cardinal

Phoenicopterus roseus

Greater flamingo

Turnix sylvaticus

Common buttonquail

Loxia leucoptera bifasciata and
Loxia leucoptera leucoptera

Two-barred crossbill and white-winged crossbill

Tyrannus forficatus

Swallow-tailed flycatcher or
scissor-tailed flycatcher

Falco tinnunculus

Common kestrel

Pyrrhula pyrrhula pyrrhula

Northern bullfinch

Spinus tristis

American goldfinch

Garrulus glandarius brandti

Brandt's jay

Setophaga townsendi

Townsend's warbler

Sturnus vulgaris

Common starling

Asio otus

Long-eared owl

Cyanocitta stelleri

Steller's jay

Ardea purpurea

Purple heron

Halcyon smyrnensis

White-throated kingfisher

Coccothraustes coccothraustes

Hawfinch

Picus viridis

Green woodpecker

Vermivora chrysoptera

Golden-winged warbler

Lanius collurio

Red-backed shrike

Phalacrocorax auritus

Double-crested cormorant

Columba palumbus

Common wood pigeon

Dendrocopos leucotos

White-backed woodpecker

Porphyrio smaragdonotus

Green-backed purple gallinule

Piranga olivacea

Scarlet tanager

Carpodacus rubicilla

Caucasian great rosefinch

Passerculus sandwichensis

Savannah sparrow

Carduelis chloris

Greenfinch